GO WILD
IN THE
WOODS

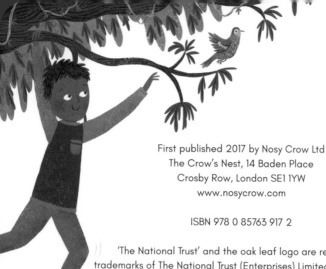

First published 2017 by Nosy Crow Ltd
The Crow's Nest, 14 Baden Place
Crosby Row, London SE1 1YW
www.nosycrow.com

ISBN 978 0 85763 917 2

'The National Trust' and the oak leaf logo are registered
trademarks of The National Trust (Enterprises) Limited (a subsidiary
of The National Trust for Places of Historic Interest or Natural
Beauty, Registered Charity Number 205846).

Nosy Crow and associated logos are trademarks
and/or registered trademarks of Nosy Crow Ltd.

Text © Goldie Hawk 2017
Illustrations © Rachael Saunders 2017

The right of Goldie Hawk to be identified as the author and Rachael
Saunders to be identified as the illustrator of this work has been asserted.

A CIP catalogue record for this book is available from the British Library.

Printed in China
Papers used by Nosy Crow are made from wood grown in
sustainable forests.

3 5 7 9 8 6 4

GO WILD
IN THE
WOODS

GOLDIE HAWK & RACHAEL SAUNDERS

nosy crow

NOTE TO GROWN-UPS

Grown-ups, be warned: this book contains sharp sticks, knives and fire!

'What?!' we hear you say . . .

But we believe it's important to teach children how to do these things correctly and with due care. Along with our instructions, we've included plenty of reminders about safety. We know that you will supervise your children properly when engaging in these potentially dangerous activities, but we also hope that this book will encourage you to join in and rediscover the fun and magic of going

WILD IN THE WOODS!

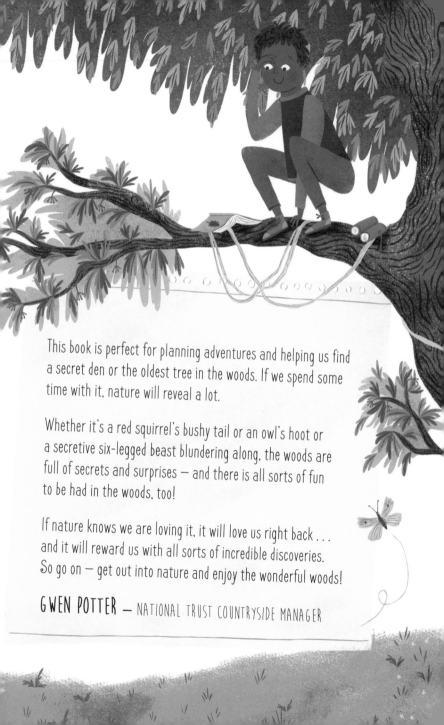

This book is perfect for planning adventures and helping us find a secret den or the oldest tree in the woods. If we spend some time with it, nature will reveal a lot.

Whether it's a red squirrel's bushy tail or an owl's hoot or a secretive six-legged beast blundering along, the woods are full of secrets and surprises — and there is all sorts of fun to be had in the woods, too!

If nature knows we are loving it, it will love us right back . . . and it will reward us with all sorts of incredible discoveries. So go on — get out into nature and enjoy the wonderful woods!

GWEN POTTER — NATIONAL TRUST COUNTRYSIDE MANAGER

CONTENTS

ARE YOU READY TO GO WILD IN THE WOODS?

You've got the ultimate team. You've found your location. Now you just need to prepare. But where on earth do you begin?

In this book, you will learn the essentials: what to pack, how to build a shelter, how to make your own tools, which wild animals to spot . . . and even how to get drinking water from your own wee! You will also learn exactly what not to do, from eating poisonous mushrooms to starting a forest fire.

This book is all about being safe and having fun. Yes, we know parents are a bit boring sometimes, but you must go camping with an adult, or several — they really can be quite useful for carrying things and digging toilets!

There are three important rules for surviving in the woods:

1. When in doubt, DON'T!
2. Always ask an adult
3. Have fun!

This book is for anyone with a thirst for adventure. You should be willing to get a bit muddy and smelly and you absolutely MUST be good at working in a team. If you would prefer to lie at home on the sofa, you might as well shut this book right now and go for a snooze.

Are you still there? Good!

LET'S GO WILD!

WHAT YOU WILL NEED IN THE WOODS
THE ULTIMATE SURVIVAL KIT

The ultimate woodland explorer needs the right gear:
not too much or you won't be able to carry it; not too
little or you won't be prepared. And you always need to
be ready for anything, so let's grab some gear and go!

WHAT TO TAKE:

- Maps
- Compass
- Penknife
- First aid kit: scissors, bandages, antiseptic wipes, gauze, tape, blister plasters, safety pins, medical tape, hydrocortisone cream, tweezers, calamine lotion, burn ointment
- Torch or headtorch
- Waterproof matches
- Portable cooking stove
- Whistle
- Thin nylon rope/paracord
- Fishing wire
- Tarpaulin
- Tent (if you're taking one)
- Sleeping bag
- Foil blanket
- Bucket
- Lightweight metal cooking grill
- Mobile phone – for emergencies only
- Duct tape
- Magnifying glass
- Cotton balls (for lighting fires or cleaning wounds)
- Snacks (cereal bars, nuts, dried fruit)
- Food
- Metal cup
- Water purification tablets
- Notebook and pencils
- Insect repellent
- Bin bags
- Flagging tape
- Gaffer tape
- Water bottle
- Wristwatch
- Aluminium foil

WHAT NOT TO TAKE:
roller skates, a trombone, a laptop, a pogo stick, a hairdryer.

WHAT TO WEAR:

- Socks (you'll need more than you think!)
- Underwear
- Walking trousers
- T-shirts
- Long-sleeved tops
- A warm jumper
- Sturdy footwear
- Gloves
- Raincoat
- Winter hat or sun hat
- Sunglasses
- Sun cream

WHAT NOT TO WEAR:
a dressing gown, a tutu, a wetsuit, high heels, a fancy hat.

How to Pack Your Rucksack

It is really, really important that you pack your rucksack correctly. If you need the toilet in the middle of the night but you can't find your torch, you will probably wake up everyone else. And if you unpack *everything*, you'll have a tricky time leaving quickly if you find yourself in trouble. Anything can happen when you're camping in the woods, from your tent leaking to animals looking for food, so you need to know where all your kit is in order to act quickly.

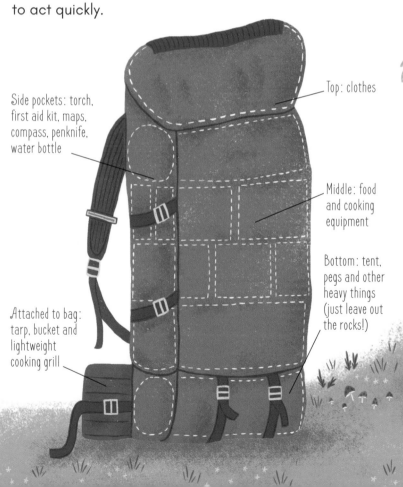

Side pockets: torch, first aid kit, maps, compass, penknife, water bottle

Top: clothes

Middle: food and cooking equipment

Bottom: tent, pegs and other heavy things (just leave out the rocks!)

Attached to bag: tarp, bucket and lightweight cooking grill

SETTING UP CAMP IN THE WOODS

The key to setting up a good camp is finding the right place! And no, you can't just camp anywhere. There are lots of rules about where you can and can't camp but the best thing to do is ask permission from the landowner beforehand.

REMEMBER
Always clean up your camp before you leave!

WHERE NOT TO SLEEP:
on a riverbank, next to your makeshift toilet, at the bottom of a hill, anywhere that has bits of tissue on the ground (probably an old camping toilet!).

PITCHING A TENT

It's a good idea to practise setting up and sleeping in your tent in your back garden before you go. This will make it much, much easier to pitch your tent when you're in the woods! Before putting up your tent, you should assess your camping ground. You don't want to topple over on a slippery slope and if you're camping at the bottom of a hill, you might end up a bit soggy. Instead, look for a level piece of ground, a good distance away from any rivers.

It is always a good idea to make sure that the doorway is facing away from any incoming wind or rain. A good view is nice too!

There are many different types of tents. Some pop up, some can be inflated and some need poles. But all should come with instructions – just remember to bring them with you!

HOW TO MAKE A SHELTER WITHOUT A TENT

No tent? No problem! If you're having issues with your tent or you need to shelter quickly from the rain, why not create your very own woodland den?

First of all, you need to work out the right shape and size for your shelter. It should be just large enough for you to lie down inside. If it's too big, there won't be enough warmth and it will take you longer to build.

There are so many different styles of shelter you can build, depending on weather conditions, how long you have to build it, and how many other people are sharing your shelter.

Of course, you shouldn't chop down living trees to make your building materials, but go in search of discarded logs and sticks, which you can chop down to the right size.

SURVIVAL TIP
Flat and dry,
happy guy.
Wet and hilly,
feeling silly!

LEAF HUT

This shelter is fairly easy to put up and is very warm because both sides are covered.

1. Find a sturdy log, around 3 metres in length.
2. Prop it up against the fork of a tree.
3. Gather lots of sticks and branches and lean these against the centre pole at an angle.
4. Pile leaves on top of these branches.
5. Weave some leafy branches in between for warmth.
6. Create your bracken mattress inside.

REMEMBER
Don't be tempted to use moss to soften your den – some mosses are very rare.

TARP

This is a great shelter when it's raining, but it is tricky to put up by yourself, so get your whole team involved when setting it up.

1. Find two trees opposite each other, around 3 metres apart.
2. Tie a rope between the trees. Sling the tarp over the rope.
3. Get a member of your team on each of the four corners of the tarp and attach pieces of rope or cord to each corner.
4. Get each member to pull on their corner so that the tarp is pulled tight and tie these ropes to branches or pegs in the ground.

TEEPEE

This is a great shelter to share with several friends.

1. Find lots of long, thin sticks.
2. Lay them all down on the ground.
3. Tie them all together at one end using rope or paracord.
4. Lift the sticks up so that they are vertical and pull them outwards, creating a cone shape.
5. Wedge the sticks into the ground so that the teepee stands without holding it; this will be a lot easier if the earth is soft.

6. To fill in the gaps, you can weave branches in and out of the sticks, or lean them up against the teepee frame, or wrap your tarp around it, securing it carefully.
7. Add extra leaves for more insulation.

Always make sure the entrance faces away from the wind, or you could have a nasty surprise!

SURVIVAL TIP
Birch bark is not only one of the best fire-lighting materials, but it can also make very effective waterproof roof tiles. Peel off bark from a fallen birch tree and layer it over your shelter.

HOW TO TIE KNOTS

It's a good idea to tie your rucksack up to a tree, so that your stuff is safe from any curious animals.

SQUARE KNOT

Also known as a reef knot, this basic knot is great if you need to tie two ropes together to form a longer rope – or indeed for tying just about anything!

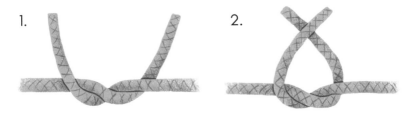

1.
2.

It's super easy to remember: right over and under left, left over and under right. Pull tight, and you're done!

3.

4.

CLOVE HITCH

This is a great knot when you need to tie something to a tree, stick or pole.

1. Wrap one end of the rope around the tree, stick or pole.

2. Cross this end up and over the wrapped part of the rope, so that it forms an X shape.

3. Loop the end over the pole once more.

4. As you bring the end of the rope back up, tuck it underneath the rope, creating another X. Pull tight.

HOW KNOT TO TIE KNOTS:
Do not tie your friend to a tree; do not tie your shoelaces together; do not attempt to lasso a grown-up.

HOW TO SLING UP A HAMMOCK

The art of slinging up the perfect hammock relies on finding two very good, strong trees that are about 1.5 metres apart. Unpack your hammock and lay it out straight. Next, you need to tie each side of the hammock to each tree, using a clove hitch knot. Make sure that your knot is tight enough by gently pressing down on the hammock. You don't want to fall out!

SURVIVAL TIP
You can make a pillow by piling lots of dry leaves into a plastic bag and covering it with a clean T-shirt.

To create a shelter over your hammock, you really need a tall friend or, failing that, you're going to have to get a leg up or climb on your rucksack. Tie a rope from up high between the two trees, using a clove hitch knot, and put some tarpaulin over the top. You will need to tie each corner to surrounding trees and branches to pull it tight.

QUICK QUIZ
Can you name five ways
a blanket could save your life?

FIVE WAYS A BLANKET COULD SAVE YOUR LIFE

1) To keep yourself warm

2) To use as a shelter

3) To use as filtering material

4) To bandage a wound if you've run out of bandages

5) To carry firewood

HOW TO MAKE TOOLS OUT OF WOOD

You can make your very own camping tools out of discarded wood and a knife. But remember: knives are VERY dangerous. ALWAYS point them away from you and if you're uncertain how to cut something correctly, get an adult to help you.

WALKING STICK

1. First, locate your stick. It should be strong and come up to your armpit.
2. Trim it down to the right size if it's too big.
3. If you want, you can (very carefully) shave the bark off using a penknife to make the stick smoother and more comfortable to grip.
4. Now you're looking like a wise, old wizard and you're all set to go!

BOW AND ARROW

1. Find some dry (but not too dry), recently dead wood for your bow. It should be around 60 cm in length.

2. Using a knife, carefully cut down the ends of your bow, so that they are thinner than the middle bit, then carve grooves at each end.

3. Find your string — you can use vines, paracord, or nylon rope.

4. Tie one end of the cord to the top of your bow, then gently bend the bow and tie the other end of the cord to the other end of your bow.

5. Find some dry, straight sticks for your arrows, about half the length of your bow and scrape off any bumps – the smoother the arrow, the quicker it will fly!

6. Carve a small notch at the back of your arrow so that it fits nicely into the string of your bow.

7. Using a knife, carefully shape the front of your arrow so that it is sharp and pointy.

8. Set up a target (this can be anything from an old stump to a rucksack) and use your bow and arrow to see if you can hit it!

WHAT NOT TO DO WITH YOUR TOOLS:
use them on animals;
use them to wake up the lazy member of your team;
use them on ANY member of your team.

CATAPULTS

1. Find a branch that is in the shape of a Y.

2. Trim it down so that the fork is about 13 cm long and the stem is about 20 cm long.

3. Scrape off all the bark, using a knife, so that your wood is nice and smooth.

4. Carve a groove into each top side of the V.

5. Locate some elastic – an elastic band will do, but you might want something thicker. It should be 45–50 cm long.

6. Tie each end of the elastic to each sides of the V, so that the elastic sits in the grooves.

7. Locate your missile (a small pebble or pine cone is best) and place it in the back of the elastic.

8. Now draw back the elastic, aim and fire!

QUICK QUIZ
Can you name ten ways
a stick could save your life?

TEN WAYS A STICK COULD SAVE YOUR LIFE

1) To create a fire by rubbing two sticks together

2) To build a shelter

3) To catch a fish

4) To build a fire for warmth and light

5) To track your route in case you get lost by cracking a stick into a V and putting it on the ground

6) To make a catapult

7) To measure the depth of water (so you don't try to cross a stream that's too deep)

8) To use it as a walking staff, so you're less likely to fall when trekking through the woods

9) To make a splint for a broken leg or finger

10) To build a makeshift fire-stove

CAMPING PEGS

Most tents come with camping pegs, but if you don't have any you can make your own using discarded wood.

1. Find some discarded sticks and cut them down so that they are around 20 cm long.

2. Carefully carve a V-shaped notch in the stick, about 5 cm from the end, so that the V is pointing towards the longer end of the stick. This notch will act as the hook on your tent peg.

3. Carve the other end of the stick into a spiky point. This will be the end that sticks into the ground.

DANGEROUS DIRT AND HELPFUL HYGIENE

Let's face it, you're going to get a bit smelly. But it's important to wash every day, especially your hands after going to the toilet, or you might become very ill. Disease spreads quickly and you do NOT want to give yourself (or your fellow campers) cholera.

If it's raining a lot, you will probably end up with wet feet, no matter how good your boots are. It's a bit like being in the bath for too long: your feet will go very crinkly and white. Soon they will get itchy and peely. Eventually, they will start rotting and going black! This is trench foot, which is very bad news indeed.

To avoid this, always sleep in a dry pair of socks. Wet feet are fine by day but if they are wet at night, you will soon have a disgusting pair of rotting feet to deal with.

HOW TO WASH IN THE WOODS

If you want to wash in the woods, you can build your very own camping shower.

THE BUCKET AND PIPING SHOWER

1. You will need a bucket or carton. Find a piece of piping for your showerhead.
2. Cut a hole into your bucket the same size as the piping, 5 cm from the bottom.
3. Push your piping into the hole and fix in place using duct tape. Fill the bucket with water, but keep your piping inside the top of the bucket.
4. Sling your bucket or carton to a tree using rope.
5. Take the piping out of the top of the bucket and enjoy your hose shower!

THE BOG-STANDARD BUCKET SHOWER

If you can't find any piping, you can go for the simple bucket shower. All you need to do is fill your container with water, stand inside it and rinse yourself – it's like a mini bathtub.

HOW TO BUILD A TOILET

If you're mid-trek and you get that funny feeling, you can just dig a small hole and cover it. But remember, never go to the loo within 30 metres of running water or lakes, or you will pollute the water – and poo-lution is a very bad thing!

If you're going to be spending several nights in your camp, it's a good idea to dig a toilet.

To do this, you will need to dig a hole roughly 100 metres from your camp (to avoid attracting unwanted visitors and for the sake of your noses!). If you're camping on a hill, build the loo below you, so you don't have a nasty bit of drainage waking you up in the night! Keep a pile of the dug-up earth next to the hole so that you can shovel some earth on top of your poo to keep it smelling okay.

SURVIVAL TIP
Instead of loo roll, you can use leaves, as long as they're not poisonous! This is much better for the environment than toilet tissue, which takes a long time to decompose.

Here are some leaves that make good loo paper: oak leaves, beech leaves and common mullein (soft and fuzzy).

oak leaf

beech leaf

common mullein

What not to use:
Stinging nettles, holly and poison ivy

stinging nettle

poison ivy

holly

FINDING YOUR WAY IN THE WOODS

HOW TO READ A MAP

Don't be scared of maps. They're not really that difficult once you understand a few facts.

KEY

Most maps have a key. This is like a code to tell you where things are. On city maps, a key will tell you where to find public toilets, car parks, cafés, restaurants and ponds. There will obviously be fewer things like this in the woods, but a key will help you find ponds, bridges and campsites.

P   car park

- - - -   railway line

river

path

picnic

camping

bridge

hedge

stone wall

fence

broad tree

conifer

flower meadow

waterfall

pond

lake

HOW NOT TO READ A MAP:
upside down,
on the toilet,
in the dark.

SCALE

It would be impossible for a map to show every place in its real size, so everything is made a lot smaller. This is called drawing something to scale. Maps have different scales but all have their scale written on the front. The scale on this map is 1:10,000 because one centimetre on the map is actually 10,000 centimetres or 100 metres in real life.

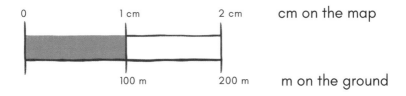

cm on the map

m on the ground

CONTOUR LINES

Because a map is flat, it would be difficult to know if there were hills without contour lines. These are drawn onto maps, so if there are lots of contour lines, you know that this area will be very hilly, but if there are little or no contour lines, the area is going to be very flat.

CROW'S
NEST
WOOD

SCALE

0   1 cm   2 cm

0   100 m   200 m

KEY

river		camping area
path		conifers
bridge		deciduous trees
wooden gate		flower meadow
hedge		pond
stone wall		lake

(This map is not to scale – it's just for fun!)

HOW TO READ A COMPASS

Modern technology means that you can usually find your way using Global Positioning Systems (GPS). But it's essential to know how a compass works, just in case you are in a remote place with no signal or your battery is low – plus, it's more fun!

There are four main points on your compass: north, south, east and west. Around the whole compass, there are little measurements, called degrees.

The most important part on the compass is the magnetic needle. It swings around the compass as you move, but the red end will always point in the direction of north and the white (or sometimes black) end will always point in the direction of south. There is also an arrow on the housing, known as the 'orientation arrow' and an arrow on the baseplate called the 'direction of travel arrow'.

If you want to walk in an exact direction, you can 'follow a bearing'. To follow a bearing, all you need to do is:

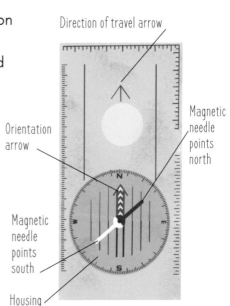

Direction of travel arrow

Orientation arrow

Magnetic needle points north

Magnetic needle points south

Housing

1. Place the compass flat on your palm, with the direction of travel arrow pointing towards where you want to go.

2. Twist your compass dial so that the orienting arrow lines up with the red end of the magnetic needle.

3. The direction of travel arrow should line up with your 'bearing' (this is the angle you want to walk in) – now you can begin your walk by following this arrow!

4. If you're worried that you're going off track, line up your orienting arrow with the needle. Whenever you do this, your direction of travel arrow will point to where you want to go (remember to keep your compass dial in the same position, though!).

HOW TO IDENTIFY CONSTELLATIONS AND USE THEM TO FIND YOUR WAY

If you're outside in the dark without a map or a compass, you can use the stars to show which way is north. It's not easy at first, but just a little bit of knowledge and practice can help you figure out which basic direction to go in.

If you're in the northern hemisphere (the half of the Earth above the equator), the most useful star is the North Star (Polaris). People often think it is the brightest star in the sky, but that's not actually true. It is fairly bright though, so you shouldn't have too much trouble finding it on a clear, moonlit night.

Polaris

The Plough

North

To find it, first you will need to find the Plough. Then imagine a straight line through the two stars that form the blade of the Plough – this will always point you to the North Star!

Then you know that if you walk towards it, you will always be heading north. If the North Star is behind you, you will be facing south.

WHAT TO SEE IN THE WOODS

WILD ANIMALS TO SPOT

DEER

Deer are shy creatures, so when you do spot them it is magical. There are lots of different types of deer, including red deer, which are large and red; fallow deer, which are slightly smaller with white speckles; and roe deer, which are even smaller with a white chin and white rump patch. Most male British deer have antlers, which they use for display and to fight with rival deer.

HEDGEHOGS

Hedgehogs are nocturnal, so they come out at night and spend the day sleeping in their nests, in shrubs or bushes. They love to eat slugs, earthworms, beetles and caterpillars. They hibernate from around November to April.

RABBITS AND HARES

It can be difficult to tell the difference between rabbits and hares. Generally, rabbits are smaller, have greyish-brown fur, shorter hind legs and long, rounded ears, whereas hares are much larger, have more ginger fur, longer hind legs and longer ears with black tips. If you spot them while they're on the move, rabbits run in bouncy hops and their short white tails stick up as a signal to other rabbits. Hares bound along very quickly by themselves, rather than in a group, so there is no need to stick up their white tails.

FOXES

Foxes look a bit like dogs, but with bushier tails and red fur, with white fur on their underside. If you live in a city or town, you may see foxes quite often, but wild foxes in the woods are more scared of people, so they are difficult to spot.

BADGERS

Badgers live in woodland holes called 'setts' and you can often find them by looking for a cluster of wide holes with straw or dried grass in a pile outside. The best time to look for them is just before sunset or about an hour before dawn. You might hear the badgers scratching or snuffling before you see them. This is when they are grooming and sniffing the air to see what's around.

BIRDS

There are all kinds of birds to spot
in the woods, from warblers and wrens
to nuthatches and tawny owls. Listen out
for different sounds, from the tapping of
a woodpecker to the rare, sweet song of
a nightingale. At night, you may hear an owl –
hoot to them and they might hoot back!

BEARS

Luckily, bears were last seen in the UK
around 1,300 years ago, but if you're
camping in a country where there
are bears, do NOT leave food
lying around. Bears love snacks,
and they are especially good at
finding any sweets you may be
hiding away. And they
may look cute
and cuddly,
but they are
actually very
dangerous!

SURVIVAL TIP
If you see a bear, stay calm.
Don't run, make sudden movements or
climb a tree. Slowly step away with your
eyes on the bear and speak in a low voice.
If it looks like it might attack, shout,
flap your arms and make
yourself look big.

OTTERS

Otters are sensitive and shy animals, so you will be lucky to spot one. Your best chance to see one is in the early morning. They live in wet places and their webbed feet, streamlined bodies and long, thick tails make them excellent swimmers. They can hold their breath under water for four minutes!

BEAVERS

Beavers are very rare, but the best time to spot them is at dusk or dawn, when they are most active. Like otters, you can find them in or near water and they are brilliant at building dams and cutting wood between their big front teeth.

WILD BOAR

Wild boar look a bit like pigs but with bulkier, hairier bodies, thick necks and very short legs. They are nocturnal and fairly rare but they can be very dangerous, so it is best to steer clear of them – especially male boars, which have sharp tusks!

VOLES

Voles look a bit like mice, but plumper, with short, hairy tails, small ears and rounded snouts. There are three different types of voles. Some live in fields, others live in gardens and some live by water, making burrows in riverbanks.

SQUIRRELS

You will probably have seen lots of grey squirrels before in towns and parks, but if you're lucky, you might spot a rare red squirrel in the woods. They are more shy than city squirrels and can most often be found in trees, looking for nuts to nibble.

PHEASANTS

Pheasants are large birds with long, exotic-looking tails. Originally from China, they are now found in many woodland areas.

CAPERCAILLIE

Capercaillie are native to the UK, and are very rare. Males have long tails, which fan out and they make strange clicking, gulping sounds.

HOW TO TRACK WILD ANIMALS

The woods are filled with beautiful animals. Whether you want to take photos or just look at them, it's really helpful if you can identify footprints and nibbled plants to know which animals have been in the area.

Can you spot chewed or scratched plants, or broken grass and shrubs? Animals eat in different ways. For example, deer rip grass out of the ground, whereas voles nibble it.

1. What can you smell?

2. Can you find any paths in tall grass?

3. Can you find any animal wee or poo? (If you do, DON'T TOUCH IT!)

HOW NOT TO TRACK ANIMALS:
Do NOT steal any animals to take home as pets. Do not pretend to be one of the animals – they will not fall for it.

REMEMBER

· Wear clothing that blends in with the woods around you

· Be as quiet as possible, so you don't scare the animals

· Stand downwind of the animals, so they can't smell you

· Never go too close to a burrow, or you might get bitten

· Step from heel to toe as it helps soften your step

· Always close gates after yourself. If an animal escapes onto a road, they might cause an accident and get hurt

· The best times to track animals are early morning, late afternoon or early evening. This is when animals are most active and their tracks are most visible

ANIMALS AND THEIR FOOTPRINTS

Look out for:

Number of toes

Size of print

Whether there are nail prints

Whether the front and back prints are the same size

Whether there are hooves or feet

Track patterns

46

TRACK PATTERN

Diagonal walker pattern: felines, canines, hoofed animals

Pacer pattern: bears, raccoons

Bounder pattern: weasels, stoats, pine martens, badgers

Hoppers: birds

Galloper pattern: rabbits, hares and most rodents

ANIMALS

Can you match the animals to the correct footprints?

BEAVER

BADGER

WILD BOAR

OTTER

RABBIT

VOLE

FOOTPRINTS

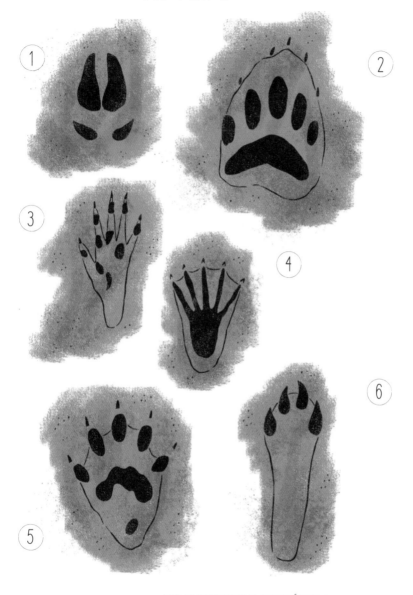

ANSWER: 1. wild boar 2. badger 3. vole 4. beaver 5. otter 6. rabbit

49

ANIMALS AND THEIR POO

Can you match the animals to the correct poo?

HARE

FOX

VOLE

DEER

BEAR

1 Tube-shaped

2 Pellet-shaped

3 Tear-shaped, tapered at one end

4 Oblong, tear-shaped

5 Very thin, small tubes

HANDY TREE GUIDE

ALDER

Alder is native and deciduous.
It can grow up to 25 metres,
has dark-green, leathery
leaves with flat ends, and can
be easily spotted by its flowers
(cylinder catkins) and fruit
(woody cones).

ASH

Ash is native and
deciduous. It can reach up
to 35 metres and grows
with other ash trees. Each
leaf is made up of several
opposite 'leaflets', and
the leaf type is called
a 'pinnate' leaf.

BEECH

Beech is native and
deciduous. It can grow taller
than 40 metres and has
hairy lime-green leaves that
become smooth and dark
as it grows older.

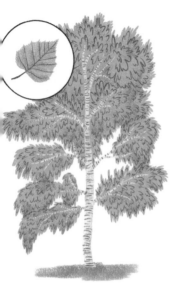

SILVER BIRCH

Silver birch is native and deciduous. It can grow up to 30 metres and prefers dry soil. It has silver bark, which sheds layers, becoming darker underneath, and its light-green leaves are triangular, with toothed edges.

HAWTHORN

Hawthorn is native and deciduous. It can grow up to 15 metres, with greyish-brown, knotted bark, thorny branches and white, scented flowers, which grow in the spring. It has small, dark-green, distinctive leaves.

MAPLE

Field maple is native and deciduous. It grows up to 20 metres and can live for 350 years. Its small leaves are dark and shiny, fanning out in five spiky points — you may recognise their shape from the Canadian flag!

ENGLISH OAK

English oak is native and deciduous. Some oaks grow to a circumference of up to 12 metres. After 40 years, it grows acorns, which fall in the autumn and are eaten by badgers and squirrels. Its green leaves are soft.

BLACK PINE

Black pine is non-native and evergreen. It can cope in dry, hot areas, as well as in snow and ice, and is easily spotted by its pine cones. It has a tall, pyramid shape, which becomes flat-topped as it gets older, creating perfect shelter for birds, deer and other mammals. It can live up to 500 years!

WHITE WILLOW

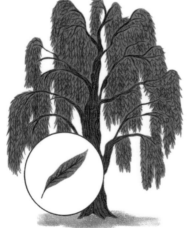

White willow is native and deciduous. It can grow up to 25 metres and is often found near rivers or streams. It has an irregular top, so it looks like it's leaning over.

HORSE CHESTNUT

Horse chestnut is non-native and deciduous. It can grow up to 40 metres, lives up to 300 years and produces conkers, which became a game almost 200 years ago.

NORWAY SPRUCE

Better known as the Christmas tree, Norway spruce is non-native and evergreen. It can grow up to 40 metres and lives up to 1,000 years! It is tall and triangle-shaped, with needle-like leaves and rough, greyish-brown bark. These trees grow wild as well as on farms, ready to be cut, taken home and decorated at Christmastime!

HOW TO EAT AND DRINK IN THE WOODS

HOW TO LIGHT A FIRE

If you want to make drinking water, cook food, or keep warm, you will need to light a fire. A word of warning before you do: you will need patience and practice, and you must remember these golden rules for safety:

1. Always keep a bucket of water or sand nearby so you can put out your fire if you need to.
2. Tie back long hair (unless you want a dodgy haircut!).
3. Make sure you always put out your fire completely when you leave the area.
4. In certain woods, you are not allowed to start fires, so always check the rules of your area before you set off.
5. If a spark lands on your clothes or you find yourself on fire, don't move! Oxygen fuels the flames and makes them bigger. Instead, STOP, DROP AND ROLL! Use a blanket to help smother the flames.
6. Never start a fire without a grown-up.

First, clear a big area of all grass, leaves and twigs. Next, create a ring of stones around where your fire will be. This will stop it spreading!

YOU WILL NEED:

1. Tinder: small, dry stuff, such as birch bark (which is very easy to set alight and is water-resistant), dry grass, dead moss, pine needles, seeds from a thistle plant, feathers, cotton balls.
2. Kindling: slightly bigger bits of dry stuff, such as pieces of split wood, dry leaves, pine cones, cotton rags.
3. Firewood: logs, fallen branches.

Make a small pile of tinder, then place the kindling in a teepee shape over it. Add logs to make a bigger teepee shape, then light the tinder with a match.

If you don't have matches, it's rather tricky to start a fire and your hands may feel as if they're going to ignite before the stick does, but there are other methods to try:

HAND DRILL

1. Find a piece of soft wood (around 30 cm long, 10 cm wide and 3 cm thick) and cut a shallow hole next to one of the long edges – don't cut all the way through!
2. Cut a V from the outer side of the shallow hole to the edge of the wood (this should go all the way through).
3. Place some tinder underneath this V.
4. Find a long, thin, hard stick and place one end in the shallow hole, holding the stick between your palms.
5. Pressing down on the stick, rotate it back and forth between your hands.
6. Eventually, the tinder will begin to smoke.
7. Blow on it gently to get your flame going – but don't get too close or your hair could catch fire too!

MAGNIFYING GLASS

1. Hold a magnifying glass, or even a lens from a pair of glasses, over dry grass, angled towards the sun.
2. You need to make the spot of light as small as you can so that all the heat goes into one area.
3. Your tinder and kindling will soon start to smoke and catch fire.

It might be hard to start a fire when you really need to, but it is also incredibly easy for forest fires to start. This is when your fire spreads to nearby trees, causing a domino effect on the entire forest.

When it's very hot and windy, these fires can spread for miles and cause massive destruction. You would NOT be very popular if you started one.

HOW NOT TO START A FIRE:
do not throw matches carelessly;
do not leave glass on dry tinder;
do not set fire to your friend.

WATER AND HOW TO FIND IT

Remember the rule of three: you can survive for three weeks without food, but only three days without water! Our bodies are 70% water, so it's really important to keep yourself hydrated. We usually get rid of three litres of water a day, but when you're out in the woods, doing more exercise and sweating more than usual, you will lose even more water.

SIGNS OF DEHYDRATION

When you're out in the woods, you need to be very careful that you don't become dehydrated. Signs of dehydration include:

- Cramps
- Feeling sick
- Headaches
- Dizziness
- Lack of energy

SURVIVAL TIP
If you start seeing elephants or giant hamburgers in the distance, you are probably VERY dehydrated and hallucinating. Your group will need to get you to a doctor quickly.

To make sure you don't get dehydrated, you need to drink plenty of water and get enough salt in you. Electrolyte sachets are very handy because you can just add them to water and they turn into a fizzy, flavoured drink (warning: this drink will NOT be very tasty but it will make you feel a lot better).

HOW TO GET DRINKING WATER FROM STREAMS

Rainwater in streams or on plants might look clean, but as soon as it has touched the ground, it can contain all sorts of germs and bacteria, including bits of animal poo and poisonous plants, which might make you very ill and dehydrated (and not a very fun camping buddy). Diseases like cholera and typhoid come from drinking bad water, so always be cautious about what you drink, no matter how thirsty you are!

To get clean drinking water, you must sterilise it before you drink it. To do this:

1. Get your fire going.
2. Make a grill or stove over the fire and place your cooking pot on top.
3. Cover the container of water you have collected with filtering material, such as a T-shirt or any type of cloth – this will get rid of any gritty bits.
4. Pour this water (with the filtering material still attached to the container) into your cooking pot.

5. Leave your water to boil for 5-10 minutes – you can speed up this step by placing some aluminium foil over your metal container.

6. Let your water cool down.

7. Once it's cool, add a chlorine or iodine purification tablet to your water and leave it for 30 minutes.

8. Now drink and enjoy!

HOW TO GET WATER FROM DEW AND MOSS

To collect dew, tie a T-shirt around your ankles and walk around on the dewy grass. The T-shirt will absorb the dew and you can then wring the water into a clean container. Finally, boil and add water purification tablets before drinking.

SURVIVAL TIP
This will NOT taste like your average glass of tap water, but it will keep you hydrated!

If it has been raining recently, you can also collect a litre of water in 20 minutes from moss. Collect bundles of moist moss and wring out the water into a clean container. Then boil and add water purification tablets before drinking.

MAKING A SOLAR STILL

You can also collect drinking water by making
a solar still. You will need: some green plants (make
sure they are NOT poisonous – see pages 70-71),
a clear plastic bag, a container.

1. Fill the plastic bag with your green plants and tie it
tightly shut.
2. Put the bag in the sun. As the plant photosynthesises,
water vapour (steam) will be produced by the leaves.
3. As the vapour touches the plastic bag, it becomes
liquid water through a process called 'condensation';
you can then collect the water in a cup or bottle.

You can also make a solar still underground by digging a hole in the ground and placing a container at the bottom of the hole.

1. Lay some plastic sheeting over the hole (this can be a cut-out plastic bag) and keep it in place using stones or earth.
2. Next, find yourself a rock and put it in the centre of the plastic, so that it's above the mug, bottle or bucket.
3. Water from the ground will condense on the bottom of the plastic sheet and drip straight into your container.
4. You can also add green plants to the hole, to collect more water.

SURVIVAL TIP
If you run out of water, sucking a small, smooth, clean pebble is a handy trick to keep saliva in your mouth and stop you getting thirsty. Just make sure you don't swallow the pebble!

QUICK QUIZ
Can you name ten ways a plastic bag could save your life?

TEN WAYS A PLASTIC BAG COULD SAVE YOUR LIFE

1) To filter water

2) To create a solar still to collect water

3) To waterproof your shelter

4) To keep your feet warm and dry

5) To turn into waterproof clothing

6) To gather tinder or food

7) To catch small fish to eat

8) To signal for help if you get lost or in trouble

9) To collect foraged food

10) To wave around to scare off wild animals

SURVIVAL TIP
Plastic bags can be dangerous. Never put them over your face or head.

HOW TO DRINK YOUR OWN WEE

Collecting drinking water from a solar still is a very slow process. To speed it up, you can add more liquid to the hole and an easy way to do this is to add your own wee in or around the hole in the ground. That's right – you can turn your wee into clean drinking water with just a plastic bag!

HOW TO FORAGE FOR FOOD

The woods are filled with edible food, from leaves and berries to mushrooms and nuts, but they also contain lots of poisonous plants and berries. Long ago, humans survived on the food they found — foraging for fruit and vegetables, as well as hunting animals and catching fish — and they knew exactly what they could and couldn't eat. Now that we're used to shopping at supermarkets, these secrets are not so well known. But to survive in the wild, you need to be able to identify what is safe to eat and what is not.

PERILOUS PLANTS

Golden rule: if you cannot identify a plant 100%, don't eat it.

Some signs that a plant is poisonous include:

- White or yellow berries
- Thorns
- Bitter or soapy taste
- Umbrella-shaped flowers
- Milky or discoloured sap
- Almond-like smell

Wolfsbane

Giant hogweed

Foxglove

Hemlock

- Clear or shiny leaves
- Leaves in groups of three
- Red splodges on stem
- Leaves with tiny hairs or fuzz
- Seeds that are purple, black or pink
- Mushrooms: 8,000 people are poisoned per year by eating mushrooms! Many mushrooms are edible, but they are very difficult to pick out because often they look identical to the poisonous mushrooms. So it's best to leave mushroom foraging to the experts!

Cuckoo pint

Deadly nightshade

GROSS GRUB

Eating bugs might sound disgusting, but they're actually a great source of protein and if you get lost in the woods with no food, they might be your only choice.

BUGS TO EAT:

ANTS: taste sweet and a little bit sour. But remember, do NOT eat red ants!

MAGGOTS: these don't taste of much but they are filled with protein.

WOODLICE: these bugs taste a bit like prawns.

GRASSHOPPERS: they taste meaty and in countries like Mexico they are considered a delicacy!

CRICKETS: like grasshoppers, they are a pleasantly meaty, crunchy snack.

BEETLES : another crunchy bug but avoid any legs or wings – there's not much protein in them and they don't taste very nice!

BUGS TO AVOID:

CATERPILLARS: the hairs might irritate your throat or mouth and some caterpillars are poisonous.

WASPS: a sting in the mouth wouldn't be the nicest mealtime treat.

SPIDERS: there's not much to them and some can bite.

FLIES AND MOSQUITOES: not only are they tiny, they also carry diseases.

And always avoid any bug that's very smelly, brightly coloured or has a sting!

SURVIVAL TIP
Some bugs have parasites. Make sure you cook your creepy crawlies well to avoid making yourself ill! This will also make them a better texture to eat.

73

HOW TO COOK YOUR FOOD
BOILING OVER THE CAMPFIRE

Boiling is great when it comes to stews, soups, pasta, rice or hot drinks.

1. Find two forked sticks around 1–1.5 metres long and wedge them into the ground, either side of your campfire, around 1 metre apart, so that the fork sides are pointing upwards.
2. Find a straight stick around 1 metre long and place this on top of the sticks, so that it is sitting in the forks.
3. Find another straight stick around 1.5 metres long and lean it against the top stick.
4. Tie your cooking pot to this stick using fishing wire.

USING A GRILL

To cook your food using a grill, you will have to add one to your kit. Luckily, they are very lightweight and can easily be tied to the back of your rucksack. To set up your grill, you can use four metal tent pegs to create a raised platform to rest your grill on. Then just add your food and cook away!

You could also just use skewers and hold them over the fire.

SURVIVAL TIP
It's a good idea to bring oven gloves – open fires get very hot and your pots and rocks will quickly get too hot to handle!

TWO-STONE OVEN

This is a great oven if you need to cook some fish, vegetables or flatbread. It acts a bit like a toastie maker, cooking your ingredients in a sandwich of hot stones.

1. Find two large and relatively flat stones.
2. Place one stone on the ground and add some small stones on top. These will create a slight platform so that the two large stones are not touching.
3. Place your second stone on top of these small stones.
4. Make a fire around the stones – this will make them very hot.
5. Carefully place your food between the stones and it will start to cook.

Alternatively, a gas hiking stove is a very easy way to cook your food. This one is definitely a job for grown-ups!

RECIPES

There are lots of fun and easy things to make over the campfire. You can wrap apples and potatoes in foil and cook them in the embers — they don't take long and they are so delicious. Here are some other recipes to try, if you don't fancy eating bugs!

SURVIVAL TIP
The most important thing to remember about eating in the woods is to always wash your hands before you cook and eat!

CAMPFIRE BREAD

Ingredients: self-raising flour (500 g), a pinch of salt, water (300–500 ml)

Method:
1. Bring your flour and salt in a plastic air-tight bag; set a bit of flour aside.
2. Gradually add water and mix everything together, massaging the bag.
3. On a clean surface (you can use your plastic bag), knead the dough by moulding it into a ball, pressing down and then reshaping it.
4. Roll the dough into a long sausage shape.
5. Find a good, clean, fresh stick and wind your dough around it.
6. Put your stick over the fire to cook.
7. After a few minutes, your dough will turn into delicious bread!

S'MORES

Ingredients: marshmallows (1 packet), digestive biscuits (1 packet), some milk chocolate (50 g or more!)

Method:
1. Find a long, thin stick and skewer it through your marshmallow.
2. Toast your marshmallow over your campfire, until it is slightly browned and nice and gooey.
3. Place a square of milk chocolate on a digestive biscuit.
4. Add your toasted marshmallow on top.
5. Place another digestive biscuit on top of your marshmallow.
6. Now eat and enjoy . . . you'll be asking for s'more!

JACKET POTATO

Jacket potatoes are the perfect campfire meal. They're warming, easy to cook and keep you full of energy.

Method:

1. First, take your potato and prod it several times with a fork to make small holes. This will make it cook more evenly and stop a messy jacket-potato explosion.
2. Next, wrap your potato tightly in two layers of aluminium foil and carefully place it in the hot embers of your campfire for 30 minutes or on your cooking grill for 40 minutes.
3. Once it is done, carefully take it out of the campfire with oven mitts or thick gloves and leave it to cool down a bit before unwrapping and eating.
4. You can add butter and cheese to your potato to make it extra tasty!

BAKED APPLES AND BANANAS

For a sweeter snack, you can cook apples and bananas in aluminium foil. Apples take 10 minutes to cook, while bananas take 5–8 minutes. Add cinnamon when they're done for extra flavour!

REMEMBER
The cooking time will vary depending on how hot your campfire is. If your potato, apple or banana isn't soft enough after these suggested times, you can always pop them back in to cook for longer.

GETTING INJURED IN THE WOODS

Anything could happen when you're living wild in the woods. You or someone in your team might get ill or fall and break a bone. Here's how to help.

BITES, STINGS AND BURNS

If you get stung by stinging nettles, look for a patch of dock leaves. They tend to grow next to stinging nettles, which is very handy because they contain a natural antihistamine, which makes itches and stings less painful.

dock leaf

SURVIVAL TIP
Try not to scratch your bite or sting — it will feel worse and could become infected.

Wasp and bee stings can be very painful at first but they can be easily treated. Hydrocortisone cream is a great thing to have in your first aid kit because it stops the sting from itching or stinging so much.

If you or your team get burnt, remove any clothing or items, such as watches, that might be covering or near the burnt area, unless the clothing is stuck to the burn – in which case, do not touch it and get help immediately!

Cool the burn with cold running water and gently rub burn ointment over it. Then attach a clean gauze bandage.

WHAT NOT TO USE: butter, tea, a dock leaf.

HOW TO BANDAGE A WOUND

1. Control bleeding by pressing or wrapping a clean cloth around the wound.
2. Gently remove any bits that are stuck in the wound.
3. Clean the wound with plain soap and clean water.
4. Press a sanitised (straight out of the wrapper) bandage to the wound.
5. If you don't have any bandages, you can use a piece of clean cloth.
6. Secure the dressing with water-resistant, non-stretch medical tape and cover it.
7. Change the dressing daily.

SURVIVAL TIP
Rubbing raw crab apple over a wound can help to heal it. Also, saliva is a very good antiseptic.

BROKEN BONES AND SPRAINS

If someone sprains an ankle or breaks a bone, they will be in a lot of pain. Do not annoy them or try to give them a relaxing massage. The best thing you can do is try to reduce the swelling. If you have something cool like a wet cloth, place this on the sprain or break. Next, you need to find some kind of support for them to lean on. Then call for help!

GETTING LOST IN THE WOODS
WHAT TO DO IF YOU GET LOST

If you get lost, don't panic. STAY STILL – if you remain where you are, chances are that whoever you were with will retrace their steps to find you. But if you run off to look for them, you will probably end up even more lost.

If you are lost with other people, the most important thing is teamwork. Even if you are scared, it can be dangerous to be selfish when you're lost. If you work as a team and remain kind and positive, you are far more likely to find your way to safety. This means sharing your food, trying to ignore your teammate's annoying humming, and NOT insisting that you know the way then marching off without listening to your team. Always stick together!

SURVIVAL TIP
If you get very cold, you can stuff dry leaves inside your jacket to keep you warm.

WHAT TO DO IF YOU GET LOST AT NIGHT

If you're lost in the dark, you can use your torch to send a Morse code SOS signal, which is three short flashes, followed by three long ones, and then three more short flashes.

S = • • •
O = − − −
S = • • •

Do NOT use your torches to have a midnight disco, or people nearby might believe that you're in trouble when you're not. You can also use a signal mirror or a large piece of aluminium foil to signal to search parties.

FIVE WAYS TO KEEP SPIRITS HIGH IF YOU GET LOST IN THE WOODS

1) Singing
2) Telling stories – but remember, not *everyone* likes ghost stories!
3) Holding a darts match – make a target and take it in turns to use a catapult to try and hit it (just don't throw them at your friends!)
4) Telling jokes
5) Having a sleeping-bag race (don't do this if it is wet or you have no food or are feeling very tired. That would just be silly.)

WONDERFUL WILD WOODS

We hope you have a wonderfully wild time in the woods. They can be a magical place, whether you're watching the sunlight filter down through the trees early in the morning or whether you're watching stars fill the sky at night.

While it's great fun to go wild in the woods, it's most important to be respectful of this beautiful space. This means following the rules, listening to your grown-ups and being careful not to disturb the environment. As the saying goes, you should leave only footprints and take only memories!

Before you leave the woods, be sure to hug a tree: the bigger the tree, the more arms you will need to hug it! Join hands with your team members and take a moment to thank the trees in the woods for a special time — who knows, maybe they can hear you?

GLOSSARY

Antihistamine cream
A cream that can soothe allergic reactions like itchiness and rashes.

Bacteria Tiny organisms that live on, in and around most living and non-living things. Some can be harmful and cause disease.

Bearing The direction in which your destination lies.

Compass A tool that uses magnetised needles to show the direction of magnetic north. It helps users to work out the direction in which they need to go.

Condensation Water that has collected on a surface due to meeting humid air.

Conifers Trees that grow cones and evergreen leaves like needles or scales. Traditionally, Christmas trees are conifers.

Constellation A group of stars that form a recognised pattern. Scientists have identified 88 constellations in the night sky.

Deciduous trees Trees that drop their leaves every year in a particular season.

Decompose To break down, decay and become rotten.

Dehydrate To feel weak or ill because you don't have enough water in your body. It can be very dangerous to be dehydrated.

Disease An illness that affects part of your body or how it works. All living things can be diseased, for example by bacteria or viruses.

Edible Something that can be eaten.

Electrolytes Salt and minerals that control the fluid balance in your body. They are important for energy and for muscles.

Evergreen trees Trees that keep their green leaves all through the year.

Forage To search for food.

Germs Very small organisms or bugs that often cause diseases.

Global Positioning System (GPS)
A worldwide system that uses satellites to allow people to work out exactly where they are, how fast they are going and what time it is.

Hemisphere One half of the earth. The equator divides our planet into northern and southern halves.

Hibernate To spend the winter months resting and sleeping. The body temperature drops and breathing slows down.

Hygiene Anything you do to keep yourself and your surroundings healthy and clean.

Morse code A way of sending messages using long and short bursts of light or sound.

Native Connected to a particular place because of having grown or been born there.

Nocturnal animals Creatures that are active at night and sleep during the day.

Orienting Working out a position relating to the points of the compass (north, south, east and west).

Parasite A living thing that lives on or in another species, using them to get food. Human parasites are often harmful and can cause diseases. Ticks are parasites.

Photosynthesis The way plants use sunlight and chlorophyll to turn carbon dioxide and water into food.

Poisonous Something that will make you ill or even kill you if you eat it.

Pollute To make something unclean, especially with harmful chemicals or waste products.

Protein A nutrient in food that is an important part of your diet. Protein gives energy. It also builds, maintains and replaces the things that your body is made from.

Saliva The watery liquid in your mouth. It helps you to taste, chew, swallow and digest your food.

Scale The ratio between real life sizes and how many times something has been shrunk to fit it on the map.

Solar still A tool that uses the sun's rays to turn salt water or unclean water into water that is safe to drink.

Sterilise To make something free from live bacteria or other tiny organisms that could cause disease.

Tarp or tarpaulin A heavy, waterproof cloth that can be used as protection from wet, windy weather.

Track pattern A series of tracks that shows an animal's steps and movements. Different animals move across the ground in lots of different ways, such as waddling, galloping and bounding.

INDEX